MY BODY Inside and Out!

What Happens When I Move?

by Ruth Owen

Consultant:

Suzy Gazlay, MA
Recipient, Presidential Award for Excellence in Science Teaching

Published in 2014 by Ruby Tuesday Books Ltd.

Editor: Mark J. Sachner
Designers: Tammy West and Emma Randall

Photo credits:
Science Photo Library: 11 (bottom), 15 (bottom);
Shutterstock: 1, 4–5, 6–7, 8–9, 10, 11 (top), 12–13, 14,
15 (top), 16–17, 18–19, 20–21, 22–23; Superstock: Cover.

Library of Congress Control Number: 2013908617

ISBN 978-1-909673-28-1

Printed and published in the United States of America

For further information including rights and permissions
requests, please contact our Customer Service Department
at 877-337-8577.

Contents

On the Move.. 4

Bones for Movement................................. 6

Joints for Movement 8

Muscles for Movement 10

Your Muscles in Action 12

Your Brain Makes It Happen 14

Puffing and Panting 16

Your Beating Heart.................................. 18

It's All About Teamwork 20

Glossary 22

Index 24

Read More..24

Learn More Online..................................24

Words shown in **bold** in the text are
explained in the glossary.

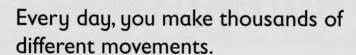
On the Move

Every day, you make thousands of different movements.

Did you know that each one begins with your **brain**?

Before you throw a ball or take a step, your brain sends instructions to your body.

Then a team of different body parts makes that movement happen. Let's check it out.

What happens when I move?

Bones for Movement

When you run, swim, or shoot a basketball, you are using your **bones**, **joints**, and **muscles**.

Your bones make a strong framework for your body called a **skeleton**.

Without your skeleton, you'd be a saggy bag of body parts that couldn't move!

Your bones are joined to each other by pieces of stretchy **tissue** called **ligaments**.

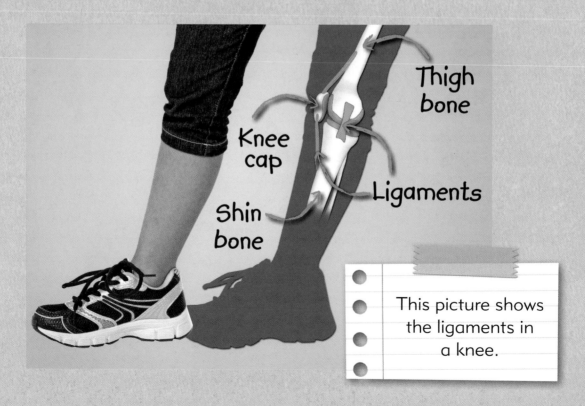

Thigh bone

Knee cap

Ligaments

Shin bone

This picture shows the ligaments in a knee.

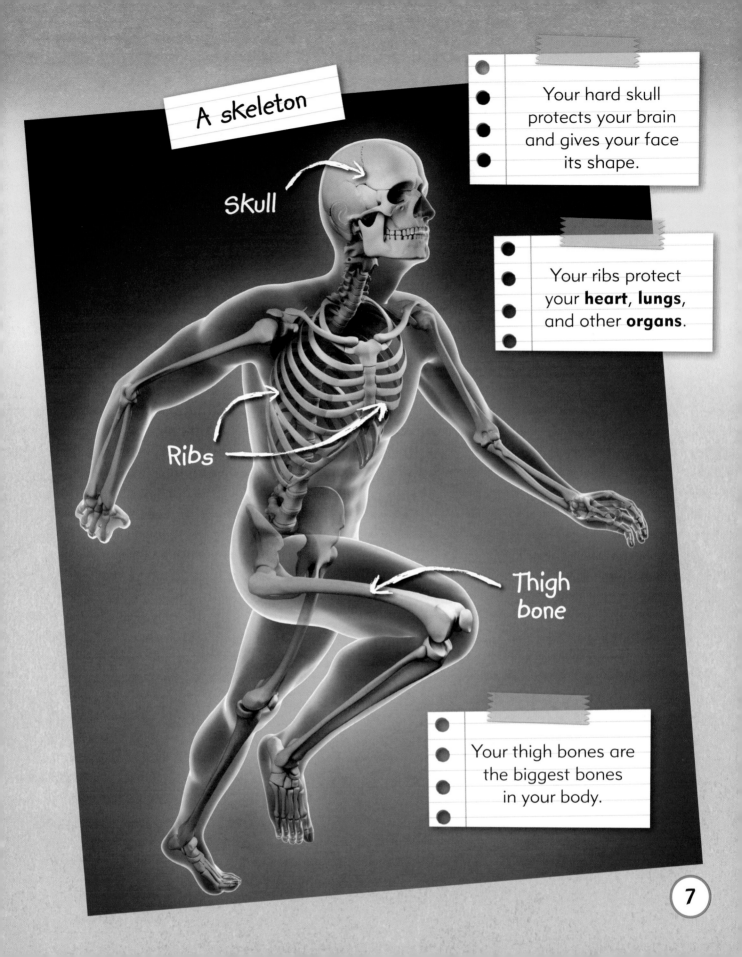

A skeleton

Skull

Ribs

Thigh
bone

Your hard skull
protects your brain
and gives your face
its shape.

Your ribs protect
your **heart**, **lungs**,
and other **organs**.

Your thigh bones are
the biggest bones
in your body.

Joints for Movement

The places where your bones meet are called joints.

Your hips, knees, shoulders, and elbows are all joints.

If you didn't have joints, your skeleton would be stiff.

You would not be able to bend your legs and fingers, turn your head, or make any other movements.

Where your leg joins to your hip, there is a ball-and-socket joint. The ball part of the bone can move forward, backward, and sideways in the socket part. It can also make a **rotating** movement.

Socket

Ball

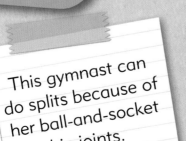

This gymnast can do splits because of her ball-and-socket hip joints.

8

Your shoulder is a ball-and-socket joint. It makes it possible to rotate, or circle, your arm to pitch a ball.

Shoulder

Elbow

Knee

Hip

Your knee and your elbow are called hinge joints. They allow your legs and arms to move in one direction and then go back again.

Muscles for Movement

Your bones and joints make movements, but what actually makes them move?

Your bones are moved, or pulled, by your muscles.

Muscles are made of tough, stretchy tissue.

There are more than 650 muscles in your body.

They are attached to your bones by strong, stretchy tissue called **tendons**.

The muscles of your face are attached to your skull and skin. When you smile or make a face, muscles pull on your lips, cheeks, and skin.

Even the smallest movement you make uses muscles. Wriggle your index finger. You've just used 17 muscles!

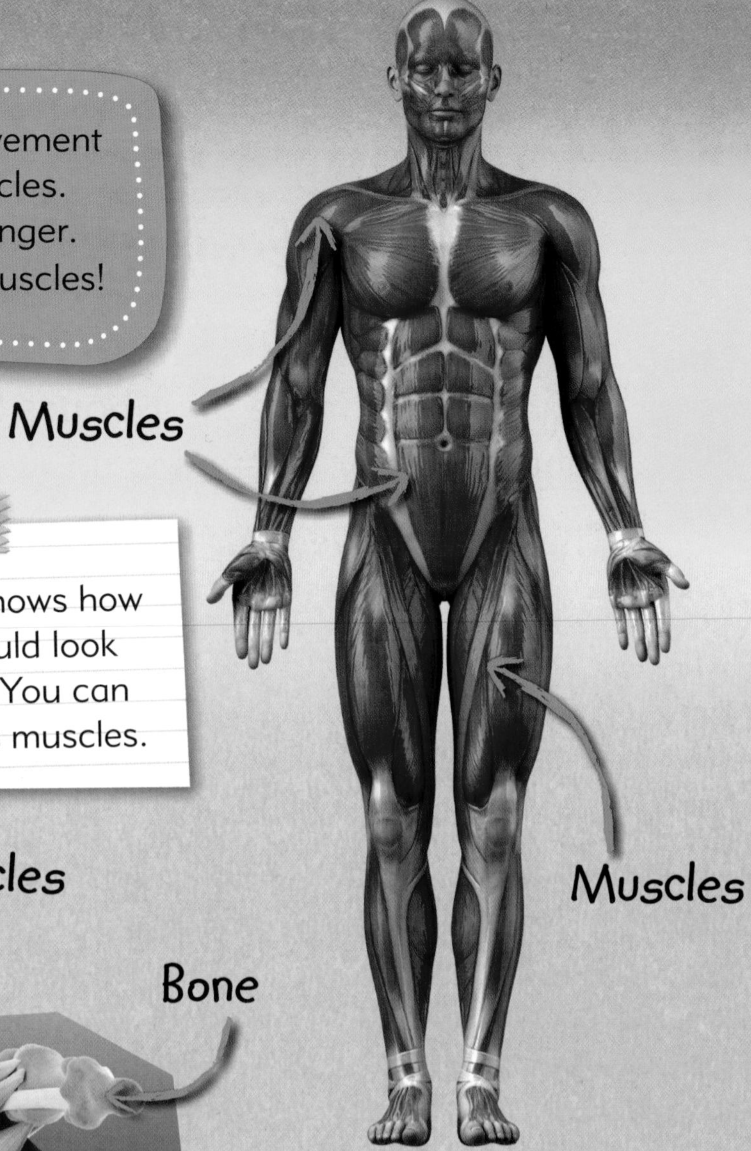

Muscles

This picture shows how a person would look without skin. You can see the body's muscles.

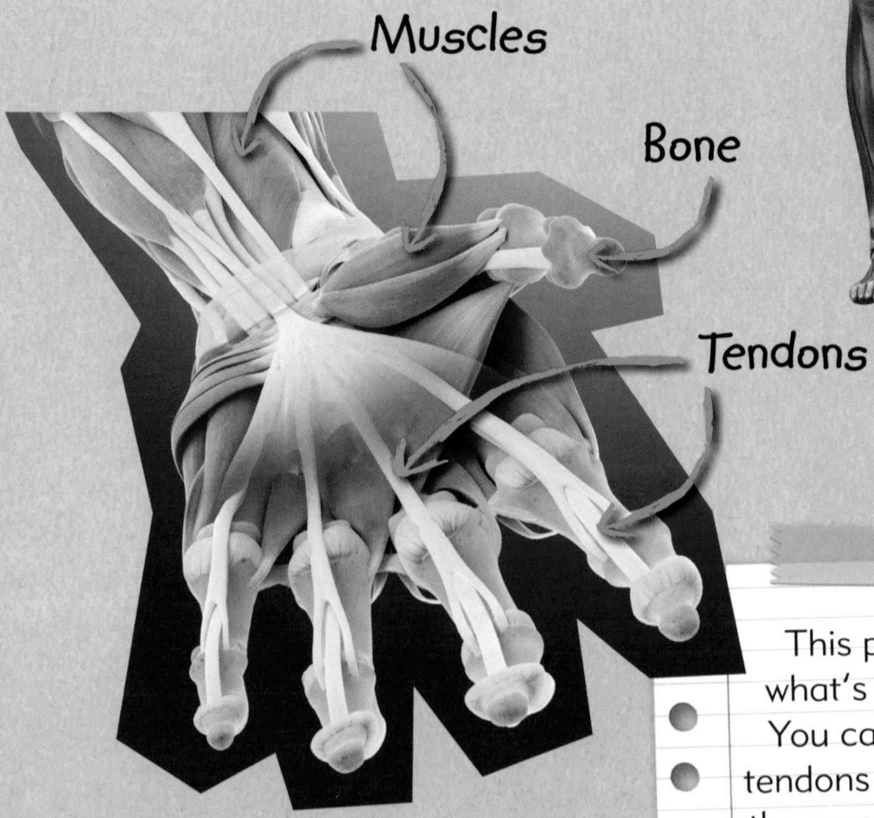

Muscles

Muscles

Bone

Tendons

This picture shows what's inside a hand. You can see how the tendons are attached to the muscles and bones.

Your Muscles in Action

Your muscles move your bones by contracting, or tightening up.

They also move your bones when they relax.

Muscles can pull bones in one direction, but they can't push them back.

So to make your bones move back and forth, your muscles work in pairs.

By contracting and relaxing as a team, a pair of muscles causes movement.

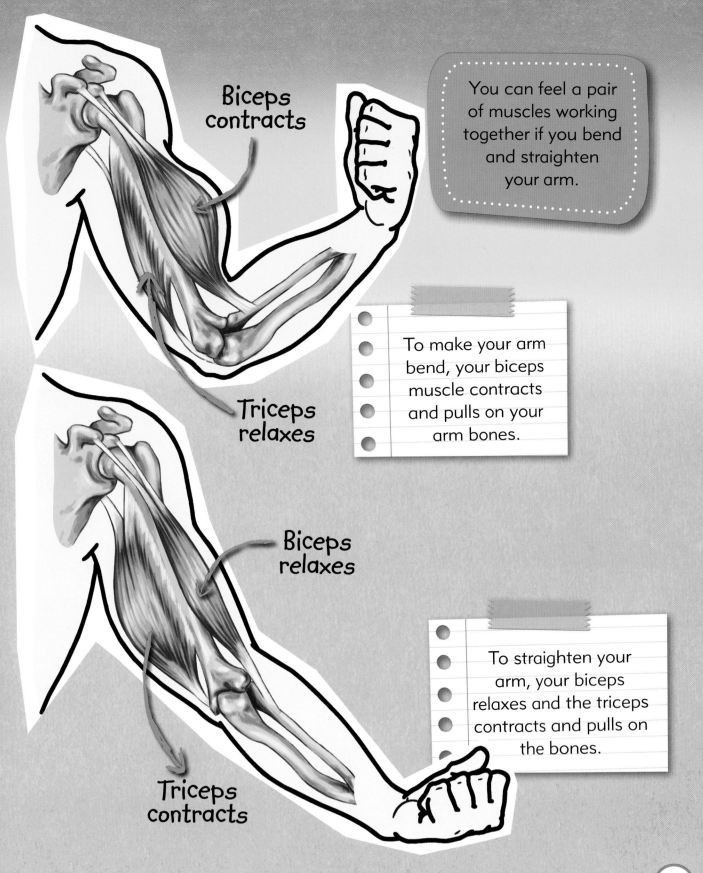

Biceps contracts

Triceps relaxes

Biceps relaxes

Triceps contracts

You can feel a pair of muscles working together if you bend and straighten your arm.

To make your arm bend, your biceps muscle contracts and pulls on your arm bones.

To straighten your arm, your biceps relaxes and the triceps contracts and pulls on the bones.

Your Brain Makes It Happen

Every movement your muscles make is controlled by your brain.

As you brush your teeth, your brain is sending instructions to the muscles in your arm, hand, and mouth.

The instructions travel from your brain down a pathway called your **spinal cord**.

Then they speed along **nerves** to the body parts that need to move.

Your brain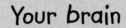

Your body parts send messages back to the brain along the nerves and spinal cord, too.

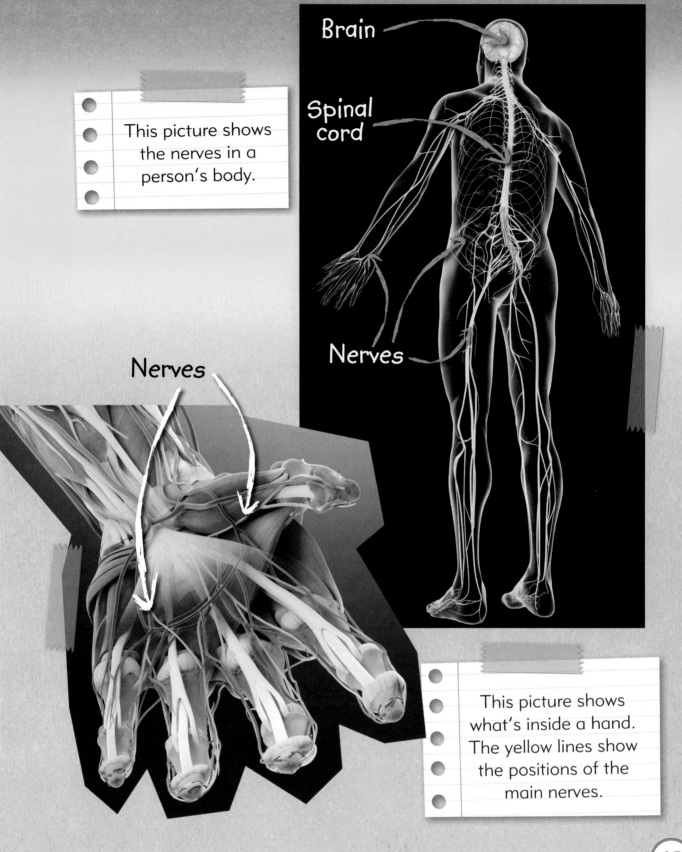

This picture shows the nerves in a person's body.

Brain

Spinal cord

Nerves

Nerves

This picture shows what's inside a hand. The yellow lines show the positions of the main nerves.

Puffing and Panting

When you're running a race, your brain tells your muscles to move your bones fast!

You won't get very far, though, unless you can breathe.

To create energy, your muscles and other body parts need a **gas** called **oxygen**.

You take in oxygen when you breathe in air through your nose and mouth.

The faster you run, the more oxygen your body needs to create energy.

So your brain tells you to breathe faster and faster until you are puffing and panting!

How does oxygen get into your body?

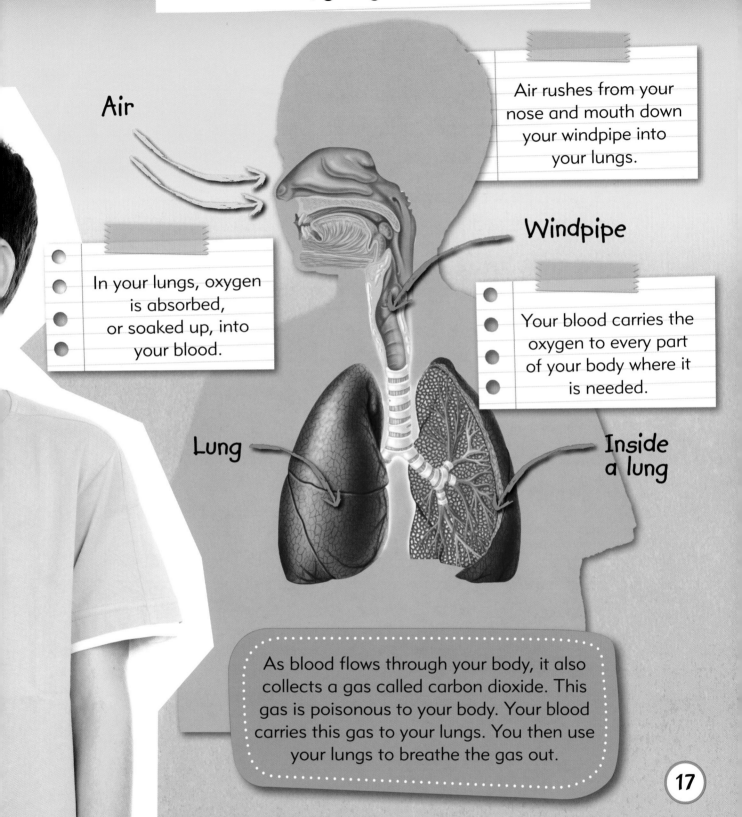

Air

Air rushes from your nose and mouth down your windpipe into your lungs.

Windpipe

In your lungs, oxygen is absorbed, or soaked up, into your blood.

Your blood carries the oxygen to every part of your body where it is needed.

Lung

Inside a lung

As blood flows through your body, it also collects a gas called carbon dioxide. This gas is poisonous to your body. Your blood carries this gas to your lungs. You then use your lungs to breathe the gas out.

17

Your Beating Heart

At the end of a race, you will probably feel your heart beating fast. Why?

It's your heart's job to pump, or push, your blood around your body.

Then your blood can carry oxygen from your lungs to your muscles and other body parts.

Your heart usually beats, and pumps, about 70 times each minute.

When you do exercise, it must beat faster to deliver more oxygen to make more energy.

That's why when you move around fast, your heart beats fast, too.

Your blood has many important jobs to do. For example, it delivers **nutrients** from your food to where they are needed in your body. Together, nutrients and oxygen give you energy.

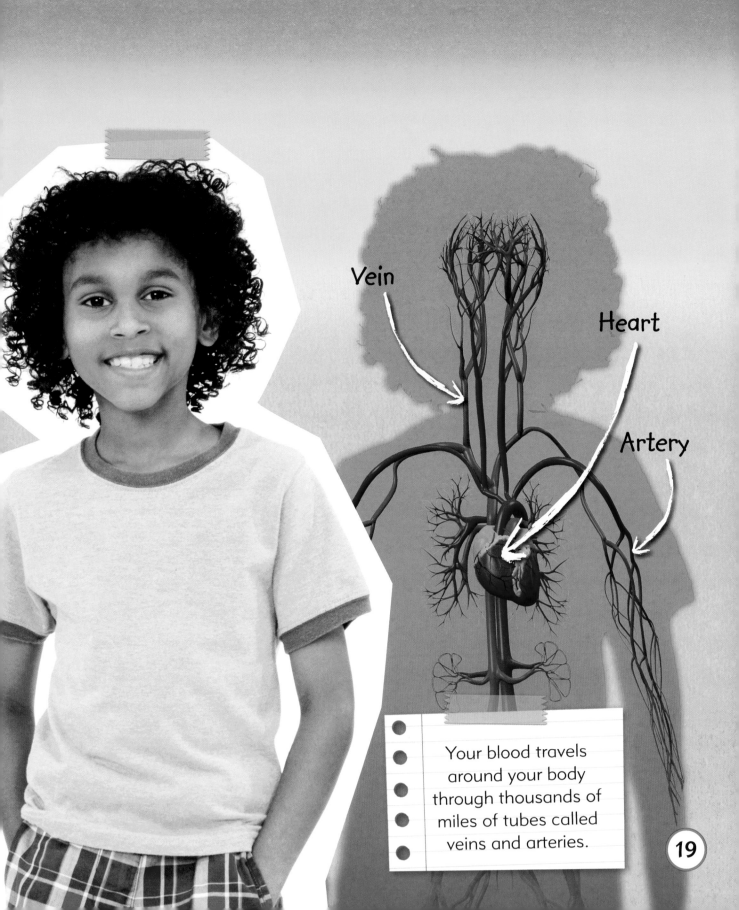

Vein

Heart

Artery

Your blood travels around your body through thousands of miles of tubes called veins and arteries.

19

It's All About Teamwork

When you learn a new swimming stroke or gymnastics move, you have to practice it.

That's because your muscles must learn what your brain is telling them to do.

Each time you practice, it helps your muscles remember.

Finally, you can speed through the water or do that tumbling move without thinking about it.

No matter how big or small the movement you make, it's all about teamwork.

Your brain, muscles, bones, and other body parts work together to keep you on the move.

Do you know how much you weigh? Half of your body's weight is your muscles.

bone (BOHN) A hard, unbending part of your body. Bones support your muscles and other body parts.

brain (BRANE) The body part that controls your senses, thinking, and movements. Messages between your brain and other parts of your body are sent and received through nerves.

gas (GASS) A substance, such as oxygen or carbon dioxide, that does not have a definite shape or size.

heart (HART) The large, muscular organ, or body part, in your chest that pumps blood throughout your body.

joint (JOYNT) A place in the body where two or more bones meet.

ligament (LIH-guh-mint) Tough, stretchy tissue that connects bones to one another.

lungs (LUHNGZ) The organs, or body parts, in your chest that collect oxygen from the air that you breathe in and pass it into your blood. They also collect carbon dioxide from your blood so that it can be breathed back out.

muscle (MUH-suhl) A part of the body that contracts, or tightens up, and relaxes to produce movement. Muscles use energy that comes from food and oxygen.

nerve (NURV) A type of cell that carries messages from the brain to every part of the body. Cells are very tiny parts of a living thing.

nutrient (NOO-tree-uhnt) A substance taken in by the body, usually through food, that the body needs to grow, get energy, and stay healthy.

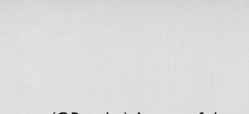

organ (OR-guhn) A part of the body, such as the heart or brain, that has a particular important job to do.

oxygen (OX-ih-jin) An invisible gas in the air that living things need to breathe.

rotating (ROH-tay-teeng) Moving in a circle.

skeleton (SKEL-ih-tuhn) The framework of bones that supports and protects your body.

spinal cord (SPY-nuhl KORD) A long bundle of nerve tissue that connects your brain with nearly every part of your body. Your spinal cord runs down your back and is protected by the bones of your spine.

tendon (TEN-duhn) Strong tissue that connects muscle to bone.

tissue (TISH-yoo) A group of connected cells in your body that work together. Cells are very tiny parts of a living thing. Your body is made of many different types of cells, including bone cells, muscle cells, and nerve cells. Muscle tissue, for example, is made up of muscle cells.

23

Index

B
ball-and-socket joints 8–9
biceps 13
blood 17, 18–19
bones 6–7, 8, 10–11, 12–13, 16, 20
brain 4, 7, 14–15, 16, 20
breathing 16–17

C
carbon dioxide 17

E
elbows 8–9
energy 16, 18

H
heart 7, 18–19
hinge joints 9
hips 8–9

J
joints 6, 8–9, 10

K
knees 6, 8–9

L
ligaments 6
lungs 7, 17, 18

M
muscles 6, 10–11, 12–13, 14, 16, 18, 20

N
nerves 14–15
nutrients 18

O
oxygen 16–17, 18

R
ribs 7

S
shoulders 8–9
skeletons 6–7, 8
skulls 7, 10
spinal cord 14–15

T
tendons 10–11
triceps 13

Read More

Williams, Ben.
Look Inside: Your Skeleton and Muscles (TIME For Kids Nonfiction Readers). Huntington Beach, CA: Teacher Created Materials (2012).

Wood, Lily.
Skeletons. New York: Scholastic (2011).

Learn More Online

To learn more about what happens when you move, go to
www.rubytuesdaybooks.com/mybodymove